# THE SPIRITED ACTOR

## Principles for a Successful Audition

**Tracey Moore-Marable**

The Spirited Actor
New York

ISBN: 0-7596-6184-7

This book is printed on acid free paper.

Edited By: Rhonda M. Jordan

1stBooks - rev. 3/18/02

"Imagination frees the spirit."

*Tracey Moore-Marable*

# Foreword

I would like to start off by congratulating Tracey Moore-Marable on successfully completing her first book. I've already accepted the fact that it won't be too much longer before I have to start sharing her with the rest of the world. I'm not happy about it, but who am to keep so many others from the world's greatest acting coach!

I first began studying with Tracey about three years ago, and I'll admit, when we first came together, I was a little cautious. I thought what could an "acting coach" actually do for me? You see, I was approaching the whole acting game with the idea that it would be second nature to me. I had been performing in front of audiences for years and expressing myself through my music for even longer. How much "coaching" did I really need? Most of the roles I had played up to that point didn't require me to "spread my acting wings" so things came pretty easy to me. Well, it wasn't long after meeting and studying with Tracey that I came to appreciate, understand and respect the art of acting. I learned that it was more about taking risks, playing roles I normally wouldn't play and pushing myself in ways I never thought imaginable. It was with Tracey's guidance that I came to trust my instincts as an actor, as an artist and as a human being. I came to understand that being an actor is a process, something that requires dedication and a lot of hard work.

Tracey has been instrumental in teaching me about the intricacies of performing in front of the camera. I NEVER set foot on a film set without her. As a musician I'm very headstrong about how I express myself. Nobody tells Busta Rhymes how to write, produce or deliver a song. But Tracey has shown me the importance of taking direction, knowing when to improvise and when not to, understanding when to listen and when to voice my own opinion about a role. This has proved invaluable to me when working with directors, writers and other artists. Tracey has also given me the courage to begin developing and writing my own projects. It's because of her encouragement and guidance that I've explored so many uncharted territories.

I can't say enough about how Tracey has shaped and influenced my artistic journey. I've learned that being an artist is all encompassing and that as I grow as an actor/writer/producer/director, I grow as a person as well. Tracey has been so many things to me - a mentor, a teacher, a friend and a spiritual guide. I am truly a testament to her methods. I only hope that other artists can begin to benefit from this handbook half as much as I have.

In closing, I would like to thank Tracey Moore-Marable once again for embracing me as her proud, humble and from what she's told me incredibly talented apprentice in this great big world of acting, writing, television and film. Personally, I feel privileged having absorbed so many different qualities at one time or another from her. Tracey is not only my acting coach, she is a dear friend who is a blessing to me and countless actors who are benefiting from The Spirited Actor philosophy.

Know this, I would never co-sign something unless it has proven itself to be official, not just for me but overall. Tracey Moore-Marable is the real thing!

Busta Rhymes.

# Dedication

This book is my gift to my Dad,
James Boston Moore II, a
truly positive person, who continues to inspire and guide me, in spirit.

Also to Michelle Thomas, a genuine
talent. Your spirit lives, sister!

Photo: Henry Adebenojo
Jewelry: Larry Patterson
Hair: Ona Locksmyths

# Introduction

When I decided to become a Casting Director, I had no idea how to approach the business, but I was determined. I browsed the Drama Book Shop in New York to collect any information on Casting Directors that I could find. I found plenty of books that gave detailed descriptions of what a Casting Director's job entails. I learned that a Casting Director is a liaison between the Director and the Talent. A Casting Director's job is to "discover" talent for the specific medium they are working in, i.e. television, film, commercials, music videos and industrials. The descriptions seemed very "clinical" and I could not find any other specific information about the actual process. Nor are there classes that you can take to "study" what a Casting Director does.

I learned very early in life not to let obstacles prevent me from achieving my goals, so I decided to call several top Casting Directors in New York to be enlightened. Well, needless to say, no one volunteered any information. I could have given up at that point, but I decided to accept the challenge and persevere. I called the same Casting Directors back and informed them that I was a student at NYU writing an article about how underrated Casting Directors are. The information came pouring out, and thus my career began. I made some mistakes along the way, but I learned from them and created a successful fifteen year career as a Casting Director that started in music videos then expanded to television, film and commercials.

I have always embraced the needs of the actor first. This is partly due to my experience as a theatrical actress in my early years growing up in San Francisco, California. I studied drama in high school and continued my education at the Pacific Conservatory of the Performing Arts in Santa Maria, California. I have never had a desire to pursue acting as a career. My dream was and continues to be a Director.

In order for actors to learn to empower themselves in an audition, they must first understand what the audition process is. Many actors have a misconception about Casting Directors making the final decision; this is not true. Once a Casting Director has presented their choices of actors to the Director then the Director makes the final decision. In most cases the Producer, Studio or Network also play a vital role in the decision making process. A Casting Director can strongly suggest or highly recommend, but it is extremely rare that it is their decision.

The casting experience has been a blessing because it has allowed me the opportunity to work with some talented people at the embryo stages of their careers. I have watched some of these actors grow into major forces in the business. I have witnessed the "highs" and "lows" throughout their journey. But, most importantly, I have come to understand the mental and physical stamina that enables them to persevere, and I feel it is my responsibility to share this knowledge with you. Whether you are just starting out as an actor or you are currently working on a series it doesn't matter because everyone can learn and grow in this business at any stage.

Let's face it, everyone at some point in his or her life has fantasized about being an actor. Whether you admit it or not, you have watched a film or television show and thought to yourself that you could perform that role. And why not, because in most peoples opinion it seems effortless, and how much work <u>really</u> goes into being an actor? The truth is that acting goes well beyond a routine "9 to 5" and those who are fortunate enough to have a career in this business have worked long and hard at perfecting their talents.

There are plenty of books on the technical aspects of acting. But, **THE SPIRITED ACTOR: Principles For A Successful Audition** uniquely addresses the personal needs of the actor, working to embellish the actor's talents while providing positive armor to all who are determined to survive and succeed as a "working" actor.

A lot of actors are not working today simply because they don't have their "acts" together. Sloppy resumes and inappropriate star photos scream "amateur" to most Casting Directors. Actors entering the audition space clueless as to what to expect are rubber stamped "rookie" or worse. This book reveals some of casting director's top pet peeves and tells what really goes on behind the scenes. It's not enough to say you want to be an actor today, you have to believe.

**The Spirited Actor: Principles for a Successful Audition** is the motivational tool that will inspire and uplift the "person" inside the actor. It will soothe the soul of the actor while they are diligently facing the "ups and downs" of the business. So often we can be motivated or heartened by stories of others trials and tribulations. **The Spirited Actor: Principles for a Successful Audition** includes such human experiences that revitalize an actor's energies and support them in their journey. This book will be an essential gift to actors from a Casting Director who views them as a true asset in this business. **The Spirited Actor: Principles for a Successful Audition** is for those who are doing it, pursuing it, wanting it, and dreaming of it.

# Contents

# 1

# Getting

# Your Foot

# In The Door

"There are three types
of people in the world:
those who make things happen,
those who watch things happen and
those who wonder what happened."

*Anonymous*

So you've taken the classes, got some great headshots and now you're ready to audition. Where do you begin? First, let's begin with a clear understanding about what an audition is. The audition process is a vehicle for actors to display their talents to "the powers that be".

These "powers" begin with a Casting Director who is a liaison between the Talent and the Director. It is the Casting Director's job to find the best talent for each project. Too many actors complain about the process, but unless you can come up with a better solution, let's just accept it and move forward.

How do you find out about auditions? The reality is that the bulk of work for actors exists in Los Angeles or New York. If you don't live there, it may be very challenging for you. Most actors who are committed to "making it" as an actor choose at some point in their lives to re-locate to New York or Los Angeles.

There are several ways to approach the audition circuit. There are various **entertainment publications** such as Backstage Magazine, The Ross Report, The Hollywood Reporter and Variety which contain information about upcoming auditions and future projects. Some of the auditions require you to come in person and some request you mail in your headshot and resume.

An **Open Call** which is often referred to as a "cattle call" means that anyone can attend and usually the lines to audition are very long. The other type of audition is a scheduled appointment. In this case you will mail in your headshot and if you are the right "type", then you will be called in for an audition with the Casting Director.

Actors need to keep abreast about the business and the "players" in the business. I strongly suggest that actors read television and film credits. It is important to know who the people behind the scenes are and the type of productions they work on. Some Directors work with the same Casting Directors on different projects. Casting Directors like to be known for their work and this can come in handy during a conversation when you are auditioning.

The most important thing to remember in an audition is to let your shining personality glow. If you have taken the time to prepare and do your homework, then you will begin to take control of your career. As you begin to evolve in this business, never neglect to **Check In With Yourself!**

**Exercise:**

Write your biography.

_____

_____

_____

_____

_____

_____

_____

_____

_____

_____

_____

_____

_____

_____

_____

_____

_____

_____

_____

**Exercise:**

What type of characters would you like to portray?

_____

_____

_____

_____

_____

_____

_____

_____

_____

_____

_____

_____

_____

_____

_____

_____

_____

_____

_____

**Exercise:**

List your favorite television shows and feature films.

_____

_____

_____

_____

_____

_____

_____

_____

_____

_____

_____

_____

_____

_____

_____

_____

_____

_____

**Exercise:**

Describe your plan for your acting career.

_____

_____

_____

_____

_____

_____

_____

_____

_____

_____

_____

_____

_____

_____

_____

_____

_____

_____

_____

**Exercise:**

List your mentors and the people who influence you.

_____

_____

_____

_____

_____

_____

_____

_____

_____

_____

_____

_____

_____

_____

_____

_____

_____

_____

_____

# 2

# Check In

# With Yourself

"If you have no confidence in self,
you are twice defeated in the
race of life.

With confidence,
you have won even before
you have started."

*Marcus Garvey*

*Tracey Moore-Marable*

Before you rehearse your acceptance speech or plan how you are going to spend your millions as a "star", I suggest you have an honest talk with yourself. If you are not someone who deals with constructive criticism well, then you might want to reconsider this business.

You need to understand that everything is based on someone else's opinion. One Director may love you while another one does not. You must learn not to take anything personal. The important thing is how you feel about yourself.

It is a fact that the audition process is intimidating and uncomfortable, but it is the only process that we have, so you must learn to maintain your power. One way an actor can give up their power is by over reacting to the "celebrity" Director or Actor who may be present in the audition space. It is wonderful to admire and respect other people's work, but remember to leave it at that. Never put anyone on a pedestal higher than yourself. Your self worth is valuable and important too. When you define your own success you don't seek validation from others.

If you want to improve your audition, then change your attitude and perception of what the audition really is. The more you know about the process, the more empowered you will feel. I would like to share this with you, I am a Casting Director, my job is to find the best talent for the Director. Without actors I don't have a job, so who really has the power? You do! So use it to your advantage and perform! Don't waste unnecessary energy trying to figure the Casting Director out or determine whether they "like" you. Your focus should be on your performance and doing your best.

When an actor enters the audition space, a Casting Director wants **you** to be the actor for the role. It is their job for those precious minutes to give actors their undivided attention. There are times when a Casting Director may be preoccupied with something, but don't let that detour your performance. Capture their attention with a dynamic performance.

This business can be very tiresome not just emotionally, but physically. It is vital for you to maintain a healthy diet and exercise

10

regimen. Being healthy can also extend your youthfulness, which is always an advantage. Put foods into your body that strengthen you rather than wear you down. By staying physically fit you gain that much needed energy during those long hours on the set. That energy will fuel you to soar because you understand that **Failure Is Lack Of Preparation!**

**Exercise:**

What are your fears?

_____

_____

_____

_____

_____

_____

_____

_____

_____

_____

_____

_____

_____

_____

_____

_____

_____

_____

**Exercise:**

Create a list of things (material or non-material) that you want.

_____

_____

_____

_____

_____

_____

_____

_____

_____

_____

_____

_____

_____

_____

_____

_____

_____

_____

_____

_____

**Exercise:**

Create a list of things you are grateful for.

_____

_____

_____

_____

_____

_____

_____

_____

_____

_____

_____

_____

_____

_____

_____

_____

**Exercise:**

Define your success.

_____

_____

_____

_____

_____

_____

_____

_____

_____

_____

_____

_____

_____

_____

_____

_____

_____

_____

_____

**Exercise:**

Write three things that you would like to change about yourself.

_____

_____

_____

_____

_____

_____

_____

_____

_____

_____

_____

_____

_____

_____

_____

_____

_____

_____

# 3

# Failure

# Is Lack Of Preparation

"There are no secrets to success.
It is a result of preparation,
hard work and learning
from failure."

*Colin Powell*

One of the biggest mistakes you can make as an actor is not preparing for an audition. The preparation needed for an audition ranges from the interpretation of the character to the appropriate attire.

Once you get the script or sides (pages from the script), I suggest that you read the material at least three times. First, find out what the story is about. Second, try to understand the relationship between your character and the other characters in the story. Finally, you need to make a choice for your character and become the character.

Remember acting is not imitating or pretending, it is re-creating the human experience. Therefore you need to pull from your own experiences or seek the information needed to create the character. For instance, if your character is in an abusive relationship and you have never had that experience, then you need to do research for your character by reading literature. Or have a conversation with a counselor who counsels people in those types of relationships. This homework will pay off in the long run because your character will become richer and more believable.

There are several schools, for instance, Stella Adler, American Academy of Dramatic Arts and Weist Barron that teach different acting techniques. It won't hurt you to take advantage of these classes because they will teach you the discipline needed to succeed in this business.

Actors often ask how to dress for an audition. You should dress according to the character. If you are auditioning for the role of a businessperson then you should not dress in a jogging suit. You need to use your best judgment in your attire. When you don't know what to wear, always go for comfort. It is a scientific fact that colors stimulate brain waves. You should find out what colors accent you the most. A Director may not always remember your name, but they will remember the color of the outfit you were wearing.

Preparing for your audition in advance can relieve you of unwanted stress and nerves. Instead of hanging out the night before an audition partying with friends, take the time to prepare. I am often in awe of actors who have a sense of urgency about "making it" in this business. My advice is to understand and appreciate the journey because every experience you have will parlay to your next.

Do whatever you need to calm yourself and relax. As you prepare for your audition, make sure you **Arm Yourself With The Right Props!**

**Exercise:**

List the acting classes that you have taken or those you would like to enroll in and why.

_____

_____

_____

_____

_____

_____

_____

_____

_____

_____

_____

_____

_____

_____

_____

_____

_____

_____

**Exercise:**

Describe what you want to gain from an acting class.

_____

_____

_____

_____

_____

_____

_____

_____

_____

_____

_____

_____

_____

_____

_____

_____

_____

_____

**Exercise:**

How much time a day do you devote to your craft?

_____

_____

_____

_____

_____

_____

_____

_____

_____

_____

_____

_____

_____

_____

_____

_____

_____

_____

**Exercise:**

What preparation do you take before an audition?

_____

_____

_____

_____

_____

_____

_____

_____

_____

_____

_____

_____

_____

_____

_____

_____

_____

_____

_____

**Exercise:**

How do you react after an audition?

_____

_____

_____

_____

_____

_____

_____

_____

_____

_____

_____

_____

_____

_____

_____

_____

_____

_____

# 4

# Arm Yourself

# With The

# Right Props

"It is through order that
the greatest things are born."

*The wisdom of the Taoists*

Like any other profession, there are certain "props" that you will need as an actor. The most important prop that you must have is your 8 1/2 x 10 black and white headshot. You will also need a resume securely attached to your headshot with your current information. I am always flattered when actors give me a picture and resume that is not attached. I appreciate the fact that people think that I am so organized. But, the reality is - *if your headshot and resume are not attached properly, e.g. stapled, glued or printed on the picture, then it could get lost or misplaced.*

Never bring your contact sheet, a Polaroid or a wallet size photo to an audition. Go through the Backstage Magazine and search for a good photographer. You can ask a fellow actor who has a headshot that you admire to give you a reference. You should also visit a photographer and view their book before you make a decision.

Study your face in the mirror with several positions so when you take your pictures you will have an idea of how you look. Your headshot must look like you! If you have recently cut your hair or gained some weight, then you need new headshots.

Your other important tool is a resume! Don't lie on your resume. Your credits should be true and accurate. I can't tell you how many times I have noticed credits on an actor's resume that were not true. I know because I cast the production or my casting friends did. Don't get caught in an embarrassing situation with false information.

I constantly remind actors to always have a monologue in their "back pocket". Why? Because you can be fabulous in an audition and the Director may ask you to do something else. How great would it be to say, "I have a monologue"!

You should have two monologues, one dramatic and the other comedic. In your spare time you need to work on these monologues and bring them to the best performance level possible. Your monologue should not be longer than two minutes.

You can also leave videotapes or voice-over demos (no longer than five minutes), but make sure the casting person can have them. Don't get in the habit of harassing the casting person for your materials back.

Set up an office space in your home and stock it with your headshots, resumes and tapes. Once a month sit down and do a mailing to Casting Directors and Agents.

Remember, if you choose to take shortcuts, you will be shortchanged because **The First Impression Is The Only Impression!**

**Exercise:**

Find a play or screenplay that you like and choose a monologue from it. Describe the character's past, present and future.

_____

_____

_____

_____

_____

_____

_____

_____

_____

_____

_____

_____

_____

_____

_____

_____

_____

_____

_____

_____

**Exercise:**

Describe what the character in your monologue was doing before his or her speech.

_____

_____

_____

_____

_____

_____

_____

_____

_____

_____

_____

_____

_____

_____

_____

_____

_____

_____

_____

**Exercise:**

What is your character's objective?

_____

_____

_____

_____

_____

_____

_____

_____

_____

_____

_____

_____

_____

_____

_____

_____

_____

**Exercise:**

Describe a resolution to your character's situation at the end of the monologue.

_____

_____

_____

_____

_____

_____

_____

_____

_____

_____

_____

_____

_____

_____

_____

_____

_____

_____

**Exercise:**

Write your own monologue.

_____

_____

_____

_____

_____

_____

_____

_____

_____

_____

_____

_____

_____

_____

_____

_____

_____

# 5

# The First Impression
# Is Your Only
# Impression

"Trust your hopes not your fears."

*David Mahoney*

When you enter an audition space, you should arrive with a pleasant attitude. You don't have to come in bouncing off the walls with a "Kool-aide" smile, but you should be polite and acknowledge everyone in the room with eye contact and a firm handshake.

Treat an audition like a job interview. Never come into the room chewing gum! Don't come in as if you just rolled out of bed. In fact, take time the night before to decide how you want to look. Make sure that you are well groomed and neat. In most auditions you are in a space with one or two other people, so be sure to check your scent.

The audition process is about talent, but it is also about personality. It is important that you speak clearly and enunciate your words during any conversation. Take the time to really think before you speak and answer questions as wisely or be as interesting as you can. I have asked actors on several occasions to "tell me something interesting about yourself?" This should be an easy thing to do because there is no dialogue to memorize, but actors continue to stumble on this. Do it now. Ask yourself the question and really think of an answer that will leave an impression.

As challenging as it may be, try to relax and let your true personality shine. In the audition Casting Directors and Directors like to get an idea of who you are. In most productions you are required to spend a great deal of time with the crew. It's important that we all feel good with each other. Casting Directors and Directors need to get a sense of your energy as a person not just as an actor.

As an actor you need to understand that you are the product. Your goods are the total package! I have auditioned incredibly talented people, but they had funky personalities. We all have bad days and that's allowed, but when it becomes a part of who you are, that's annoying. Casting decisions can come down to who is easiest to work with.

You have to love being an actor because the journey is not always pleasant. Instead of absorbing that negative energy, be happy that you have an opportunity to showcase your talent and do what you love. When you enter the audition space, use common courtesy and allow yourself to relax as you **Find Your Comfort Zone!**

**Exercise:**

Write something interesting about yourself?

_____

_____

_____

_____

_____

_____

_____

_____

_____

_____

_____

_____

_____

_____

_____

_____

_____

**Exercise:**

Describe how you feel when you receive a compliment.

_____

_____

_____

_____

_____

_____

_____

_____

_____

_____

_____

_____

_____

_____

_____

_____

_____

_____

_____

**Exercise:**

Describe how you feel when you receive constructive criticism.

_____

_____

_____

_____

_____

_____

_____

_____

_____

_____

_____

_____

_____

_____

_____

_____

_____

_____

_____

_____

**Exercise:**

Write the names of the people who support you and how it makes you feel.

_____

_____

_____

_____

_____

_____

_____

_____

_____

_____

_____

_____

_____

_____

_____

_____

_____

_____

*Tracey Moore-Marable*

## Exercise:

How do you reward yourself when you complete an audition?

_____

_____

_____

_____

_____

_____

_____

_____

_____

_____

_____

_____

_____

_____

_____

_____

_____

_____

_____

# 6

# Find Your

# Comfort Zone

"Nothing can dim the light
which shines within."

*Maya Angelou*

As an actor, there will be times when you feel as if you are riding an emotional roller coaster. The reality is that you are going to go through "ups" and "downs" in this business. But how do you maintain a sense of balance and stability? How do you avoid the frustrations and rejections yet deal with the egos that exist?

I suggest you find a place deep inside yourself where you can retreat to collect your strength and energy. Belief in yourself is the first step. Regardless of what others say about your talent, you must be able to stand by it and defend it at all times.

Learn to uplift yourself with daily affirmations that motivate you through your journey. Carry a pocket journal with some of your favorite quotes. Create a strong vision in your mind of where you would like to go in your career. Most importantly, define your success! It may be a room full of shoes, a brand new car or the fact that you have peace of mind knowing that your bills are paid on time. It doesn't matter what it is as long as you've defined it for yourself.

You need to surround yourself with positive and supportive people. I feel that when you share experiences with others who understand, it will only add to your growth as a person and as an actor. Knowing that other actors become nervous during auditions is refreshing. You're not alone. It's not about being nervous, it is about how you handle it. Take those nerves and control them, incorporate them into the sides for the audition. For instance, the character may be upset or angry, learn to funnel those nerves into the character. You may decide to pace around the room in character and let those nerves settle.

You can gain comfort as an actor when you know that you are doing everything possible to move your career along. This means that you are taking classes, working on your monologue and giving your best in your auditions. You should understand that learning is a continuous process and you will grow into a better actor. Be patient with yourself and know that you are where you are because it is where you're supposed to be.

Being an actor is just a part of your life, you should have other things that you embrace to enrich your life. Try to maintain peace in your life with the comfort of knowing that there is a role out there for you and **Time Is Of The Essence!**

*Tracey Moore-Marable*

**Exercise:**

Describe how you spend your time alone.

_____

_____

_____

_____

_____

_____

_____

_____

_____

_____

_____

_____

_____

_____

_____

_____

**Exercise:**

You say you have an abundance of talent, how did you discover it?

_____

_____

_____

_____

_____

_____

_____

_____

_____

_____

_____

_____

_____

_____

_____

_____

_____

_____

**Exercise:**

Define your vision of where you would like to go in your career.

_____

_____

_____

_____

_____

_____

_____

_____

_____

_____

_____

_____

_____

_____

_____

_____

_____

_____

**Exercise:**

Write a list of prayers or affirmations that help you through your "down" times.

_____

_____

_____

_____

_____

_____

_____

_____

_____

_____

_____

_____

_____

_____

_____

_____

_____

_____

*Tracey Moore-Marable*

## Exercise:

Describe how you keep fit mentally, physically and spiritually.

_____

_____

_____

_____

_____

_____

_____

_____

_____

_____

_____

_____

_____

_____

_____

_____

_____

_____

# 7

# Time Is Of

# The Essence

"Some are born great,
some achieve greatness
and some have greatness
thrust upon' em."

*Anonymous*

I often find myself searching for more time to accomplish things I need to take care of. My daily planner is a lifesaver because it allows me time to schedule as well as organize my day. Casting Directors are always on a schedule and being late for an audition is not going to score any points for you. A lot of the anxiety that I have experienced from actors during an audition has come from their tardiness.

When you arrive late for your audition, you don't allow yourself time to relax and collect your thoughts before entering a room. You may not even have time to look over the material, so you feel rushed or unprepared. Avoid that situation by planning ahead. Of course some situations cannot be avoided, but leave enough room in your schedule for train, bus or traffic delays.

Once you have arrived in the audition space, be considerate of everyone's time. Don't go into "monologues" about unrelated issues or ramble endlessly about nothing. If you have any questions make sure that they are brief and to the point. There are probably other people behind you waiting to get in and the Casting Director has a schedule.

I enjoy planning my audition schedule because I looked forward to meeting new actors and catching up with familiar ones. When I schedule my auditions, I don't want to keep anyone waiting. It's nerve wracking enough to go through the process, but to sit around and wait can drive you crazy! But, the truth is waiting is a part of the audition process, so be prepared. Patience is a virtue.

Actors need to get in the habit of working with someone else's schedule. When you are hired for a job, time plays a very important role. Even the Director works by the clock. Your time to be on the set (Call Time) could be at 6:00 a.m. and several miles from your home. You should rise early in order to be there on time. If you are not an early riser this could be a challenge. I suggest you get in the habit now because on a set, time is money, and no one wants to go over budget because of a tardy actor.

When an actor understands and respects time, it assures the Casting Director and the Director that they are dealing with a professional. Then you are ready to proceed to **Lights, Camera, Action!**

**Exercise:**

How do you prepare for an audition?

_____

_____

_____

_____

_____

_____

_____

_____

_____

_____

_____

_____

_____

_____

_____

_____

_____

**Exercise:**

If you find yourself in a "rut," how do you bring yourself out of it?

_____

_____

_____

_____

_____

_____

_____

_____

_____

_____

_____

_____

_____

_____

_____

_____

_____

_____

_____

**Exercise:**

How do you react when you're nervous?

_____

_____

_____

_____

_____

_____

_____

_____

_____

_____

_____

_____

_____

_____

_____

_____

**Exercise:**

Describe a defining moment in your life.

_____

_____

_____

_____

_____

_____

_____

_____

_____

_____

_____

_____

_____

_____

_____

_____

_____

_____

**Exercise:**

List your special abilities, e.g. eating fire.

_____

_____

_____

_____

_____

_____

_____

_____

_____

_____

_____

_____

_____

_____

_____

_____

_____

# 8

# Lights,

# Camera,

# Action

"Shoot for the moon.
Even if you miss it
you will land among the stars."

*Les Brown*

The moment that you were waiting for has finally arrived, it is time to perform! Correct me if I'm wrong, but this is what the "big hoopla" is all about, right? Absolutely! You have prepared for this moment and it is the only thing that matters now. So, why are you preoccupied by other things?

First of all, unless you have a personal relationship with the Casting Director or Director you will never figure them out. Your performance is the only thing you have control over, so stay in the moment. Remember to listen very carefully and apply whatever information is given to your performance.

If you don't understand the direction, then be honest and say so. The worst mistake you can make in an audition is not following direction. If you are not given any information, then trust your instincts! Make a firm choice with your character and be consistent. I continue to stress to actors that a Director has a vision or a feeling about who they would like to see in a role, but you have the power to change their minds based upon your performance. That's why there are erasers, liquid paper and delete buttons. Changes are constantly being made.

I have witnessed several instances where an actor did a fabulous job and the Director had to reconsider the role. In the film "An Officer and a Gentleman" Louis Gossett Jr. won an Oscar for Best Supporting Actor, a role which was written for a white actor. This is just one of many examples that what is written is not always written in stone. Actors have the power to change the image of defined characters.

When you are in an audition space do your job! Perform! Don't talk about doing it or hope to do it, just do it! This is your moment to shine and you should take advantage of it. Make your audition standout by pacing yourself, listening to direction and giving a great performance!

When all is said and done, you achieved your goal with a dynamic performance and **That's A Wrap!**

**Exercise:**

Describe your attitude when you enter an audition.

_____

_____

_____

_____

_____

_____

_____

_____

_____

_____

_____

_____

_____

_____

_____

_____

_____

_____

_____

**Exercise:**

Are you prepared for your leading role?

_____

_____

_____

_____

_____

_____

_____

_____

_____

_____

_____

_____

_____

_____

_____

_____

_____

**Exercise:**

Can you honestly say that you take direction well?

_____

_____

_____

_____

_____

_____

_____

_____

_____

_____

_____

_____

_____

_____

_____

_____

_____

_____

_____

**Exercise:**

List the Directors you would like to work with and why.

_____

_____

_____

_____

_____

_____

_____

_____

_____

_____

_____

_____

_____

_____

_____

_____

_____

_____

**Exercise:**

List the Casting Directors that you would like to display your talents to and why. (Suggestion: read television and film credits).

# 9

# That's A Wrap

"It's better to be looked over
than overlooked."

*Mae West*

It's over, relax and breathe! I applaud you for your courage, but most importantly I salute your true commitment to being an actor. Not everyone can stand in front of a bunch of strangers and display their talents so brilliantly as you just did. Take a minute and embrace yourself for your efforts, because it's important to let yourself know how proud you are.

Don't ruin this moment by rehashing the audition or judging your performance. The bottom line is your opinion doesn't matter. It's the opinion of the Casting Director that matters, then the final decision lies with the Director, Producer, Studio and /or Network.

Don't waste time, let it go. There are plenty of things for you to do, like organizing a professional mailing system for your headshot and resumes, taking classes or scheduling your next audition. Before that, remember to take a minute to reward yourself. It doesn't have to cost you a dime. You could take a walk through the park and reconnect with the beauty around you. Or you could visit a bookstore and browse through your favorite section.

I have a friend who constantly reminds me when "stress" tries to enter my life, that I am only making movies not discovering the cure to cancer. This statement is embedded in my mind because it puts my job into perspective.

I love my job, but it is merely a part of my life, it is not my life. I have a wonderful husband and two spectacular children who are my life. When you understand what is truly important in your life everything that you desire has a way of falling into place, trust me. Play hard, study, stay focused on your goals, but most of all enjoy life because it's easy to miss the great things that make life worthwhile.

I have a great collection of books that inspire me to be persistent in this business. I understand the power behind words. Entertain your mind with positive words that create the life you want as an actor. Don't always rely on "Hollywood" or other entities to create your career. As an actor, I believe you are a creative being and the possibilities are endless. Write a one-person show, direct a one-act play or start a theatre company. You have the power to create. Take your career in your own hands and explore the different opportunities that you can create for yourself.

Learn from each audition and finally take along with you some **Food For Thought!**

**Exercise:**

List your positive words.

_____

_____

_____

_____

_____

_____

_____

_____

_____

_____

_____

_____

_____

_____

_____

_____

_____

_____

**Exercise:**

If you were not getting paid to perform, would you do it anyway?

_____

_____

_____

_____

_____

_____

_____

_____

_____

_____

_____

_____

_____

_____

_____

_____

**Exercise:**

What type of things (other than acting) would you like to do?

_____

_____

_____

_____

_____

_____

_____

_____

_____

_____

_____

_____

_____

_____

_____

_____

_____

_____

_____

**Exercise:**

Write a one-act play.

_____

_____

_____

_____

_____

_____

_____

_____

_____

_____

_____

_____

_____

_____

_____

_____

_____

_____

_____

**Exercise:**

Write your Tony, Emmy or Oscar acceptance speech.

_____

_____

_____

_____

_____

_____

_____

_____

_____

_____

_____

_____

_____

_____

_____

_____

_____

_____

_____

# 10

# Food For

# Thought

"You must act as if
it is impossible to fail."

*Ashanti proverb*

I respect and apprecilove actors. I believe that you are a valuable asset to the production. But you should know that there are not a lot of positive egos floating around in this business. As a result, some people tend to "power trip" and lose their minds. I strongly encourage you to stay grounded and treat people as you expect to be treated. This business is based on relationships, therefore it pays to establish as many good ones as you can.

After your audition understand this, if you are talented you will be remembered. Whether you get the role or not, Casting Directors talk to other Casting Directors, Agents and Directors. Before you know it a whole bunch of people are talking about you, and you are not even aware of it. How refreshing is that to know?

I have been very fortunate to watch several actors in the "embryo" stages of their careers. I can honestly say that these people stayed passionate, consistent and determined. They never lost sight of their goals. If they did have "down" times, they didn't allow those times to keep them down. They rose up even more determined to succeed and you can too! I can't tell you when that role is going to be yours, but I can tell you if you truly apply yourself, the role will be yours.

I have met so many wonderful people through my experiences in this business and it has truly been a blessing. I've felt their love and support every step of the way. When you allow those energies to enter your life, you have no choice but to soar. I challenge you as a beginning actor, working actor or just someone who has a curiosity about acting: dream with the belief that whatever you desire you can achieve. When doubts and fears enter your mind erase them and continue to move forward. There will be times when you question why you want to be actor. You must continually remind yourself of the "gift" that you possess and know in your heart that you truly want it. Feel secure about yourself and your talents, but most importantly follow your heart because it will never lead you astray. Act because you love it and watch the rewards flow!

**Exercise:**

Are you prepared for the long haul of an actor's life?

_____

_____

_____

_____

_____

_____

_____

_____

_____

_____

_____

_____

_____

_____

_____

_____

_____

**Exercise:**

Write an affirmation about your talents. Recite it everyday.

_____

_____

_____

_____

_____

_____

_____

_____

_____

_____

_____

_____

_____

_____

_____

_____

_____

_____

*Tracey Moore-Marable*

**Exercise:**

How do you feel when you see a fellow actor working more than you?

_____

_____

_____

_____

_____

_____

_____

_____

_____

_____

_____

_____

_____

_____

_____

_____

**Exercise:**

Remind yourself daily of why you want to be an actor.

_____

_____

_____

_____

_____

_____

_____

_____

_____

_____

_____

_____

_____

_____

_____

_____

_____

**Exercise:**

Write a letter to yourself and list your desires for the coming year. Store it away and open it a year from now.

_____

_____

_____

_____

_____

_____

_____

_____

_____

_____

_____

_____

_____

_____

_____

_____

_____

_____

# **Affirmations**

*Tracey Moore-Marable*

## 1   Getting Your Foot In The Door

"There are three types of people in the world; those who make things happen, those who watch things happen and those who wonder what happened."

*Anonymous*

## 2   Check In With Yourself

"If you have no confidence in self, you are twice defeated in the race of life. With confidence, you have won even before you have started."

*Marcus Garvey*

## 3   Failure Is Lack Of Preparation

"There are no secrets to success. It is a result of preparation, hard work, learning from failure."

*Colin Powell*

## 4   Arm Yourself With The Right Props

"It is through order that the greatest things are born."

*The wisdom of the Tao*

## 5   The First Impression Is Your Only Impression

"Trust your hopes not your fears."

*David Mahoney*

## 6   Find Your Comfort Zone

"Nothing can dim the light which shines within."

*Maya Angelou*

## 7   Time Is Of The Essence

"Some are born great, some achieve greatness and some have greatness thrust upon' em."

*Anonymous*

## 8   Lights, Camera, Action

"Shoot for the moon. Even if you miss it you will land among the stars."

*Les Brown*

## 9   That's A Wrap

"It's better to be looked over than overlooked."

*Mae West*

## 10  Food For Thought

"You must act as if it is impossible to fail"

*Ashanti proverb*

*Tracey Moore-Marable*

# Check List:

# Principles for

# A Successful Audition

**Make sure you have answered these questions before each audition.**

1   Do I have a pleasant and positive attitude?

2   Do I truly believe in my talents as an actor?

3   Have I taken the time to prepare for this audition?

4   Do I have any questions about the character or the "sides" that I am reading for?

5   Does my picture really reflect me as I am today?

6   Is the information on my resume current and accurate?

7   Am I currently involved in a project that I need to tell the Casting Director about?

8   Do I feel relaxed and focused before I enter the audition ?

9   Am I prepared to give a dynamic performance?

10  Do I trust that there is a role is out there for me?

## Thank You (for real!)

Thank you Mom, Dad, Jean, my brothers James and Barry my sister-in-law Nicole, Virginia my niece Ciara, nephews Sebastian and Alexis for your true love and support. I know you thought I was crazy, but knowing that you were on my side provided me with strength that I am truly grateful for!

Thank you Maurice, my partner in life and my biggest fan! I love and appreciate your words and your joyous way.

Thank you Radiance, my shining star! I am proud to have a dynamic daughter and friend. Your strength is an inspiration!

Thank you Myles, my little man. I am so glad to have given birth to such a strong person. Keep growing and laughing.

Thank you Carol, my best friend in the whole wide world, Sheila, my sister/cousin, you're always there, Paula, for teaching me how to pray, Glinda, for shaping me as a teenager, Walter, for the trip to L.A. (that's where I discovered my dream), Anita, for the love songs, Kerry and Ruth for your conversation, Francyne, for being you, Ileta and Jay, for your spirits. Thank you to the Moores and Woodards, the foundation of who I am.

Thank you to the Marables, Pearl, George, Micheal, Michelle, Michele, John, Rachel, Justin and Kayla.

Thank you Aiyana for never letting me down. You are more than a "baby-sitter"! (smile) And let's not forget mommy, Deborah Peterson for your love.

Thank you Rhonda, for taking the chance and letting me fly. I am so blessed!

Thank you Busta Rhymes for being incredibly talented and allowing me to be present in your space. I love the journey.

Thank you Kellita Smith, my movie star sistah, for grounding me with balance and peace.

Thank you Richard Mair and Kim Williams, my L.A. crew for the fun!

Thank you Stephanie Tavares-Rance for your honesty.

Thank you Marilyn Sue, we love you!

Thank you Pierre V, for your talents and your belief in this book, you made it happen! Thank you Michael Valdez for helping me complete my vision. You and your nickel were right on time!

Thank you Butch Robinson, for your faith in me and my first job!

Thank you Eve for being you!

Thank you to my writing mentors LaJoyce Brookshire, Seth Rosenfield and Andy Stein, your guidance is a lifesaver.

Thank you Lana Garland for being my rock.

Thank you Mona Scott for trusting your instincts and the rest of The Violator crew, Chris Lighty, Tania Wesley, Laura Ciocia, Simone, Nadia, Georgina, Don Raj and Akinah.

Thank you Lowell Williams "we are only making movies".

Thank you Jae Jae Simmons for our "sistah thang".

Thank you Phynjuar for you true energy.

Thank you Kevin Harewood for being a constant in my life.

*Tracey Moore-Marable*

Thank you Daryl Sydnor it all started with jokes.

Thank you Kyla Upshaw for your kind heart and bouncing spirit.

Thank you Matthew St. Patrick for allowing me to experience your journey.

Thank you Diane Bailey and Soneni Smith for your encouragement.

Thank you Barbara Freeman, for all your support and love, and Glen for keeping the door open.

Thank you Shirley Faison for being a spectacular person in every way.

Thank you Mr. Louis Rosier for allowing me to shoot my first short film in your laundromat.

Thank you Missy Elliott, Faith Evans, Renee Neufville, Darius Rucker (Hootie and the Blowfish), Nelly, Melissa Phillipan, Rah Digga, Spliff Star, Q-Tip, Vinnie (Naughty By Nature), Charise (Changing Faces), Chico DeBarge, Taj (SWV), Fat Man Scoop, Monica Calhoun, muMz, Tyson Beckford, Steph Lova, Kittie, Ms. Jones and Ray Allen our sessions were brilliant.

Thank you Marie Brown for your encouragement to write in the first place.

Thank you Mark Breland for your dedication.

Thank you Anna Marie Horsford for your friendship.

Thank you Mr. and Mrs. Halfhide, my spiritual couple.

Thank you to all the Producers and Directors who gave me a shot!

Thank you to all my friends at MTV, VH-1 and HBO.

Thank you Rich Murray and the "Snipes" crew, I had a ball. Also, Roger Bobb your vision is invaluable.

Thank you to my teachers, your knowledge was put to the test and I survived.

Thank you to all the people in my life who have helped me along the way: Ingrid Strugis, Andrea and Lamont Crawford, Charlotte & Chris Bauer, Gypsy, Kevin Thigpen, Rodd Garr, Richard Whitten, Robbie Todd, Morgan Spirlock, Ona "The Locksmyth", Sharron Cannon, Rolando Hudson, Estella Greene, Dave Chappelle, Shonette, Esther Swann, John Shea, Frank Sweeney and my Pagent Crew, Jacqueline Rhinheart, Gwendelyn Quinn, Bethann Hardison, Tracey Kemble, Joan Fields, Tracey McGraw, Kristi McCormick, Lance Gatewood, Edgar Clarke, Divine, Ruthie, Beau, Jason Steinberg, Brian Jones, Brenda Benton, Jill Douglass, Mike Colon, Rachel Weintraub, LaShawn Browning, Gayle King, Nikki and the sistahs at Oxygen Network, George Jackson, Maro Haile, Albert Kemson, Gabriel Cassieus, Euricka, Angelo Elerbee, Walter and Kandia Mudu, Larry Kennar, Bryon Thierry, Ian Gelfand, Larry and Sharon Patterson, Lavor Postell, David Wilson, and of course Stackhouse. I wanted to list you all, but that's a book within itself. Next time, I promise!

Thank you to all the actors who have touched my spirit, this is for you!

*Tracey Moore-Marable*

# Selected Bibliography

My sources for the various quotes used throughout this book are from:

You're the Best!
(Peter Pauper Press, Inc 1994)

Positive Thoughts:
Living Your Life to the Fullest
(Armand Eisen 1995)

The Great American Bathroom Book
(Compact Classics, Inc. 1993)

# About the Author

Tracey Moore arrived in New York City to pursue a directing career, but she was suddenly sidetracked by the many opportunities that she discovered. He first venture was CEO of "The Jokes On You!" Inc., an ensemble of actors who performed practical jokes for hire. Through the success of her company, she developed lasting relationships with various actors who were anxious to be a part of this wacky production.

After five years of performing jokes, a director noticed the bulging files that Tracey had and asked her for a casting favor. "Find a void, fill it," says Moore-Marable and so Tracey Moore Casting was born. Tracey has gone on to cast for feature films such as "Just Another Girl on the I.R.T.", "New Jersey Drive" and "A Brother's Kiss". As Extras Casting Director, Tracey cast for the popular Fox show "New York Undercover". Her commercial credits include; Nike, Sprite, Coca-Cola, New York Times, Miller Lite, Pontiac and Taco Bell to name a few.

In her "spare" time, Tracey enjoys speaking to students at various colleges. She has lectured at Howard University, Long Island University, CW Post, Georgia State University and Loyola Maramount University. She also teaches an audition technique class called "The Spirited Actor" and she conducts private coaching sessions with musical artists such as Busta Rhymes, Missy Elliot, Eve, Nelly, Chico DeBarge, Renee (Zhane), Faith Evans, Q-Tip, Darius Rucker (Hootie and the Blowfish).

Tracey realized that she was not sidetracked in her career, but she was merely experiencing the full scope of her journey. Being a Casting Director has allowed Tracey to explore the talents that exist in this business and the opportunity to work with various actors. So Tracey decided to finally pursue her dream of directing. With a small budget, a dedicated crew and lots of love, Tracey made her directorial debut with an up and coming artist named Blac Dyemond and a cameo with Samuel L. Jackson. Tracey plans to direct her featured film entitled ***Honest Lies*** in the Fall of 2002 in San Fransisco, CA.

Tracey has written a monthly column for Black Talent News entitled Casting Corner since September 1995. Other articles written were for Essence and the BET Magazine. Between coaching Busta Rhymes on "Shaft", Tracey co-wrote a short film with Busta for HBO entitled "Sounds of New York", produced by Madonna.

Tracey coached Busta in a Gus Van Sant film, "Finding Forrester", N.A.R.C. with Ray Liotta and Halloween 8 with Jamie Lee Curtis.

Tracey coached multi-platinum recording artist, Nelly on his first starring role in "Snipes" directed by Rich Murray. What does the future hold for Tracey? "I don't know what will come next because I know that life is right now, so I'm going to live in every moment of it!" laughs Moore-Marable.

Printed in the United States
141977LV00005B/1/A

9 780759 661844